Privacy Policy Template
(2023 Edition)

VISIT US ON THE INTERNET:

www.privacyblast.com

PLEASE LET US KNOW HOW WE'RE DOING:

contact@privacyblast.com

Disclaimer

Please note that the following privacy policy template is legal information not legal advice.

Privacy Blast is a maker of legal guides and do-it-yourself legal forms. Privacy Blast is not a law firm and does not provide legal advice. This website is purely the provision of legal information and not legal advice for specific cases. This website is not intended to create an attorney-client relationship and all readers should not act upon this information without seeking professional counsel.

Instructions

Privacy Policy template and Cookie Policy template are do-it-yourself, fill-in-the-blank.

Just look for variables in brackets and replace based on the specifications of your website or app.

For example, search for and replace variables within the templates that begin with "[%_"

Privacy Policy Template

Privacy Policy

Effective Date: [%_DATE_%]

This Privacy Policy describes our policies and procedures on the collection, use and disclosure of Your Personal Data when You use the Service and tells You about Your privacy rights and how the law protects You.

We use Your Personal Data to provide and improve the Service. By using the Service, You agree to the collection and use of Personal Data in accordance with this Privacy Policy.

Interpretation and Definitions

Interpretation

The words of which the initial letter is capitalized have meanings defined under the following conditions. The following definitions shall have the same meaning regardless of whether they appear in singular or in plural.

Definitions

For the purposes of this Privacy Policy:

- **Account** means a unique account created for You to access our Service or parts of our Service.
- **Company** (referred to as either "the Company", "We", "Us" or "Our" in this Privacy Policy) refers to [%_COMPANY_%].
  - For the purpose of the GDPR (General Data Protection Regulation), the Company is the Data Controller.
- **Cookies** are small files that are placed on Your computer, mobile device or any other device by a website, containing the details of Your browsing history on that website among its many uses.
- **Data Controller**, for the purposes of the GDPR (General Data Protection Regulation), refers to the Company as the legal person which alone or jointly with others determines the purposes and means of the processing of Personal Data.
- **Do Not Track** (DNT) is a concept that has been promoted by US regulatory authorities, in particular the U.S. Federal Trade Commission (FTC), for the Internet industry to develop and implement a mechanism

for allowing internet users to control the tracking of their online activities across websites.

- **Personal Data** is any information that relates to an identified or identifiable individual.
  - For the purposes for GDPR (General Data Protection Regulation), Personal Data means any information relating to You such as a name, an identification number, location data, online identifier or to one or more factors specific to the physical, physiological, genetic, mental, economic, cultural or social identity.
  - For the purposes of the California Privacy Law (as defined below), Personal Data means any information that identifies, relates to, describes or is capable of being associated with, or could reasonably be linked, directly or indirectly, with You.
  - For the purposes of U.S. state-specific privacy laws in Colorado, Virginia, Connecticut, or Utah, Personal Data may be modified by applicable U.S. state law.
- **Sale**, for the purpose of the California Privacy Law (as defined below), means selling, renting, releasing, disclosing, disseminating, making available, transferring, or otherwise communicating orally, in writing, or by electronic or other means, Personal Data to another business or a third party for monetary or other valuable consideration.
  - For the purposes of U.S. state-specific privacy laws in Colorado, Virginia, Connecticut, or Utah, Sale may be modified by applicable U.S. state law.
- **Sensitive Personal Data** may include Personal Data revealing racial or ethnic origin, religious beliefs, a mental or physical health condition or diagnosis, sex life or sexual orientation, or citizenship or citizenship status; genetic or biometric data that may be processed for the purpose of uniquely identifying an individual; or Personal Data from a known child.
  - For the purposes of U.S. state-specific privacy laws in Colorado, Virginia, Connecticut, or Utah, Sensitive Personal Data may be modified by applicable U.S. state law.
- **Service** refers to the Website.
- **Service Provider** means any natural or legal person who processes the data on behalf of the Company. It refers to third-party companies or individuals employed by the Company to facilitate the Service, to provide the Service on behalf of the Company, to perform services related to the Service or to assist the Company in analyzing how the Service is used.

- For the purpose of the GDPR (General Data Protection Regulation), Service Providers are considered Data Processors.
- **Usage Data** refers to data collected automatically, either generated by the use of the Service or from the Service infrastructure itself (for example, the duration of a page visit).
- **Website** refers to [%_COMPANY_%], accessible from www.[%_COMPANY_%].com
- **You** (referred to as either "You" or "Your" in this Privacy Policy) means the individual accessing or using the Service, or the company, or other legal entity on behalf of which such individual is accessing or using the Service, as applicable.
  - Under GDPR (General Data Protection Regulation), You can be referred to as the Data Subject or as the User as You are the individual using the Service.

Collecting and Using Your Personal Data

Types of Data Collected

Personal Data

While using Our Service, We may ask You to provide Us with certain personally identifiable information that can be used to contact or identify You. Personally identifiable information may include, but is not limited to:

- [%_add_types_of_personal_data_if_applicable_%]

When You pay for a product and/or a service via bank transfer, We may ask You to provide information to facilitate this transaction and to verify Your identity. Such information may include, without limitation:

- [%_add_types_of_personal_data_if_applicable_%]

Usage Data

Usage Data is collected automatically when using the Service.

Usage Data may include information such as Your Device's Internet Protocol address (e.g. IP address), browser type, browser version, the pages of our Service that You visit, the time and date of Your visit, the time spent on those pages, unique device identifiers and other diagnostic data.

When You access the Service by or through a mobile device, We may collect certain information automatically, including, but not limited to, the type of mobile device You use, Your mobile device unique ID, the IP address of Your mobile device, Your mobile operating system, the type of mobile Internet browser You use, unique device identifiers and other diagnostic data.

We may also collect information that Your browser sends whenever You visit our Service or when You access the Service by or through a mobile device.

Information from Third-Party Services

The Website integrates some services provided by third parties. We may share some of Your Personal Data with these suppliers so they can provide their services, including analyzing data, marketing support, customer and/or User profiling, business development, and customer service.

Please note, the terms and privacy policies of such third parties may apply to You as well, in particular: [%_add_third_party_service_if_applicable%].

Tracking Technologies and Cookies

[%_add_section_if_applicable_%]

We use Cookies and similar tracking technologies to track the activity on Our Service and store certain information. Tracking technologies used are beacons, tags, and scripts to collect and track information and to improve and analyze Our Service.

You can instruct Your browser to refuse all Cookies or to indicate when a Cookie is being sent. However, if You do not accept Cookies, You may not be able to use some parts of our Service.

Cookies can be "Persistent" or "Session" Cookies. Persistent Cookies remain on Your personal computer or mobile device when You go offline, while Session Cookies are deleted as soon as You close Your web browser.

We use both session and persistent Cookies for the purposes set out below:

[%_the_below_section_is_for_example_%]

- **Necessary / Essential Cookies**
    - Type: Session Cookies
    - Administered by: Us

- - Purpose: These Cookies are essential to provide You with services available through the Website and to enable You to use some of its features. They help to authenticate users and prevent fraudulent use of user accounts. Without these Cookies, the services that You have asked for cannot be provided, and We only use these Cookies to provide You with those services.
- **Cookies Policy / Notice Acceptance Cookies**
  - Type: Persistent Cookies
  - Administered by: Us
  - Purpose: These Cookies identify if users have accepted the use of cookies on the Service.
- **Functionality Cookies**
  - Type: Persistent Cookies
  - Administered by: Us
  - Purpose: These Cookies allow us to remember choices You make when You use the Service, such as remembering Your login details or language preference. The purpose of these Cookies is to provide You with a more personal experience and to avoid You having to re-enter Your preferences every time You use the Service.

Tracking and Performance Cookies

- Type: Persistent Cookies
- Administered by: Third-Parties
- Purpose: These Cookies are used to track information about traffic to the Website and how users use the Service. The information gathered via these Cookies may directly or indirectly identify You as an individual visitor. This is because the information collected is typically linked to a pseudonymous identifier associated with the device You use to access the Website. We may also use these Cookies to test new advertisements, pages, features or new functionality of the Service to see how our users react to them.

For more information about the cookies we use and Your choices regarding cookies, please visit our Cookie Policy or the Cookies section of our Privacy Policy.

Use of Your Personal Data

The Company may use Personal Data for the following purposes:

- [%_add_purposes_if_applicable_the_below_section_is_for_example%]
- **To provide and maintain our Service**, including to monitor the usage of our Service.
- **To manage Your Account:** to manage Your registration as a user of the Service. The Personal Data You provide can give You access to different functionalities of the Service that are available to You as a registered user.
- **For the performance of a contract:** the development, compliance and undertaking of the purchase contract for the products, items or services You have purchased or of any other contract with Us through the Service.
- **To contact You:** To contact You by email, telephone calls, SMS, or other equivalent forms of electronic communication, such as a mobile application's push notifications regarding updates or informative communications related to the functionalities, products or contracted services, including the security updates, when necessary or reasonable for their implementation.

We may share Your Personal Data in the following situations:

- [%_add_the_ways_personal_information_may_be_shared_%]

Retention of Your Personal Data

The Company will retain Your Personal Data only for as long as is necessary for the purposes set out in this Privacy Policy. We will retain and use Your Personal Data to the extent necessary to comply with our legal obligations (for example, if we are required to retain Your data to comply with applicable laws), resolve disputes, and enforce our legal agreements and policies.

The Company will also retain Usage Data for internal analysis purposes. Usage Data is generally retained for a shorter period of time, except when this data is used to strengthen the security or to improve the functionality of Our Service, or We are legally obligated to retain this data for longer time periods.

Transfer of Your Personal Data

Your information, including Personal Data, is processed at the Company's operating offices and in any other places where the parties involved in the processing are located.

It means that this information may be transferred to — and maintained on — computers located outside of Your state, province, country or other governmental jurisdiction where the data protection laws may differ than those from Your jurisdiction.

Your consent to this Privacy Policy followed by Your submission of such information represents Your agreement to that transfer.

The Company will take all steps reasonably necessary to ensure that Your Personal Data is treated securely and in accordance with this Privacy Policy and no transfer of Your Personal Data will take place to an organization or a country unless there are adequate controls in place including the security of Your data and other personal information.

Disclosure of Your Personal Data

Business Transactions

If the Company is involved in a merger, acquisition or asset sale, Your Personal Data may be transferred. We will provide notice before Your Personal Data is transferred and becomes subject to a different Privacy Policy.

Law enforcement

Under certain circumstances, the Company may be required to disclose Your Personal Data if required to do so by law or in response to valid requests by public authorities (e.g. a court or a government agency).

Other legal requirements

The Company may disclose Your Personal Data in the good faith belief that such action is necessary to:

- Comply with a legal obligation
- Protect and defend the rights or property of the Company
- Prevent or investigate possible wrongdoing in connection with the Service
- Protect the personal safety of Users of the Service or the public
- Protect against legal liability

Security of Your Personal Data

The security of Your Personal Data is important to Us, but remember that no method of transmission over the Internet, or method of electronic storage is 100% secure. While We strive to use commercially acceptable means to protect Your Personal Data, We cannot guarantee its absolute security.

Detailed Information on the Processing of Your Personal Data

Service Providers have access to Your Personal Data only to perform their tasks on Our behalf and are obligated not to disclose or use it for any other purpose.

[%_category_of_service_provider_%]

[%_description_of_cataegory_service_provider_%]

- **[%_name_of_service_provider_%]**
  - [%_information_about_service_provider_%]

GDPR Privacy

Legal Basis for Processing Personal Data under GDPR

We may process Personal Data under the following conditions:

- **Consent:** You have given Your consent for processing Personal Data for one or more specific purposes.
- **Performance of a contract:** Provision of Personal Data is necessary for the performance of an agreement with You and/or for any pre-contractual obligations thereof.
- **Legal obligations:** Processing Personal Data is necessary for compliance with a legal obligation to which the Company is subject.
- **Vital interests:** Processing Personal Data is necessary in order to protect Your vital interests or of another natural person.
- **Public interests:** Processing Personal Data is related to a task that is carried out in the public interest or in the exercise of official authority vested in the Company.

- **Legitimate interests:** Processing Personal Data is necessary for the purposes of the legitimate interests pursued by the Company.

In any case, the Company will gladly help to clarify the specific legal basis that applies to the processing, and in particular whether the provision of Personal Data is a statutory or contractual requirement, or a requirement necessary to enter into a contract.

Your Rights under the GDPR

The Company undertakes to respect the confidentiality of Your Personal Data and to guarantee You can exercise Your rights.

You have the right under this Privacy Policy, and by law if You are subject to the GDPR, to:

- **Request access to Your Personal Data.** The right to access, update or delete the information We have on You. Whenever made possible, You can access, update or request deletion of Your Personal Data directly within Your account settings section. If You are unable to perform these actions Yourself, please contact Us to assist You. This also enables You to receive a copy of the Personal Data We hold about You.
- **Request correction of the Personal Data that We hold about You.** You have the right to have any incomplete or inaccurate information We hold about You corrected.
- **Object to processing of Your Personal Data.** This right exists where We are relying on a legitimate interest as the legal basis for Our processing and there is something about Your particular situation, which makes You want to object to our processing of Your Personal Data on this ground. You also have the right to object where We are processing Your Personal Data for direct marketing purposes.
- **Request erasure of Your Personal Data.** You have the right to ask Us to delete or remove Personal Data when there is no good reason for Us to continue processing it.
- **Request the transfer of Your Personal Data.** We will provide to You, or to a third party that You have chosen, Your Personal Data in a structured, commonly used, machine-readable format. Please note that this right only applies to automated information which You initially provided consent for Us to use or where We used the information to perform a contract with You.
- **Withdraw Your consent.** You have the right to withdraw Your consent on using Your Personal Data. If You withdraw Your consent, We may not

be able to provide You with access to certain specific functionalities of the Service.

Exercising of Your GDPR Data Rights

You may exercise Your rights of access, rectification, cancellation and opposition by contacting Us. Please note that we may ask You to verify Your identity before responding to such requests. If You make a request, We will try our best to respond to You as soon as possible.

You have the right to complain to a Data Protection Authority about Our collection and use of Your Personal Data. For more information, if You are in the European Economic Area (EEA), please contact Your local data protection authority in the EEA.

California Privacy

Your rights under the California Consumer Privacy Act ("CCPA"), as amended by the California Privacy Rights Act ("CPRA") (collectively, the "California Privacy Law")

Under this Privacy Policy, and by law if You are a resident of California, You have the following rights:

- **The right to notice.** You must be properly notified which categories of Personal Data are being collected and the purposes for which the Personal Data is being used.
- **The right to access and the right to request.** The California Privacy Law permits You to request and obtain from the Company information regarding the disclosure of Your Personal Data that has been collected in the past 12 months by the Company or its subsidiaries to a third party for the third party's direct marketing purposes.
- **The right to say no to the Sale or Sharing of Personal Data.** You have the right to ask the Company not to sell or share Your Personal Data to third parties. You can submit such a request by visiting our "Do Not Sell My Personal Information" section or web page.
- **The right to limit the use and disclosure of Sensitive Personal Data.** You have right to limit how the Company uses and discloses Your Sensitive Personal Data. To exercise Your right to limit, You may submit a

request to the Us by visiting our "Limit the Use of My Sensitive Personal Information" section or web page.

- **The right to know about Your Personal Data.** You have the right to request and obtain from the Company information regarding the disclosure of the following:
  - The categories of Personal Data collected
  - The categories of sources from which the Personal Data was collected
  - The business or commercial purpose for collecting, selling, sharing, or disclosing the Personal Data
  - The categories of third parties with whom We sold, share, or disclosed Personal Data for a business or commercial purpose
  - The specific pieces of Personal Data we collected about You, subject to certain exceptions under applicable law
- **The right to delete Personal Data.** You have the right to request the deletion of Your Personal Data that have been collected in the past 12 months.
- **The right not to be discriminated against.** You have the right not to be discriminated against for exercising any of Your rights, including by:
  - Denying goods or services to You
  - Charging different prices or rates for goods or services, including the use of discounts or other benefits or imposing penalties
  - Providing a different level or quality of goods or services to You
  - Suggesting that You will receive a different price or rate for goods or services or a different level or quality of goods or services.
- **The right to correct inaccurate Personal Data.** You have the right to request that we correct any of Your Personal Data that we maintain about You, taking into account the nature of the Personal Data and the purposes of the processing of Your Personal Data.
- **The right to appeal.** You have the right to appeal any decision or indecision related to the exercise of any right You are granted under California Privacy Law.

Exercising Your California Privacy Law Data Protection Rights

You do not need to create an account with us to exercise Your California Law privacy rights. To exercise the rights described above, please submit a request to us by emailing: [%_email_%].

To exercise Your right to know, delete, or correct Your Personal Data as described above, we need to verify Your identity or authority to make the request and confirm the Personal Data relates to You. We will not provide You with Personal Data if we cannot verify Your identity or authority to make the request and confirm the Personal Data relates to You. Making a verifiable request does not require You to create an account with us. We use Personal Data provided in a verifiable request solely to verify the requestor's identity or authority to make the request.

These requests may be made only by You, Your parent, guardian (if You are under 18 years or age), conservator, a person to whom You have given power of attorney pursuant to California Probate Code sections 4000 to 4465, or an authorized agent. As permitted under California Law, we may request that an individual submitting a request on behalf of an individual submit proof that they are an authorized agent of the subject individual, as well as verify the individual's identity. To protect Your Personal Data, we reserve the right to deny a request from an agent that does not submit adequate proof that You authorized them to act for You.

We are only required to respond to a verifiable right to know request twice within a 12-month period. The verifiable request must provide sufficient information to allow us to verify You (or an authorized agent) are the person about whom we collected Personal Data.

We do not charge a fee to process or respond to Your verifiable request unless it is excessive, repetitive, or manifestly unfounded. If we determine that the request warrants a fee, we will tell You why we made that decision and provide You with a cost estimate before completing Your request.

Once we have verified a request from a California resident, we will confirm receipt of the request within 10 days and explain how we will process the request. We will then respond to the request within 45 days. We may require an additional 45 days (for a total of 90 days) to process Your request, but in those situations, we will provide You a response and explanation for the reason it will take more than 45 days to respond to the request. Our responses will include required information under California Law.

Do Not Sell My Personal Information

We do not sell personal information. However, the Service Providers we partner with (for example, our advertising partners) may use technology on the Service that "sells" personal information as defined by the California Privacy Law.

If You wish to opt out of the use of Your personal information for interest-based advertising purposes and these potential Sales as defined under the California Privacy Law, You may do so by following the instructions below.

Please note that any opt out is specific to the browser You use. You may need to opt out on every browser that You use.

Colorado, Connecticut, Virginia, Utah - Additional Privacy Rights

Your rights under privacy law in Colorado, Connecticut, Virginia, or Utah

In addition to the rights available to residents of California, residents of Colorado, Connecticut, Utah or Virginia, may also have the rights described below in this section with respect to the Personal Data that we collect about You. This section applies solely to eligible residents of Colorado, Connecticut, Utah or Virginia. Any terms not defined in this section have the same meaning as defined under applicable Colorado, Connecticut, Utah and Virginia privacy law, including the Colorado Privacy Act, Connecticut Data Privacy Act, Utah Consumer Privacy Act and Virginia Consumer Data Protection Act.

- **The right to correction.** You have the right to request a business that possesses inaccurate Personal Data about You to correct such inaccurate Personal Data, taking into the account the nature of the Personal Data and the purposes of the processing of the Personal Data.
- **The right to notice.** Businesses must inform You at or before the point of collection what categories of Personal Data will be collected and the purposes for which these categories will be used.
- **The right to access.** You have the right to request that a business disclose the categories of Personal Data collected; the categories of sources from which Personal Data is collected; the business or commercial purpose; the categories of third parties with which the business shares Personal Data; and the specific pieces of Personal Data the business holds about You. If a business sells Personal Data or discloses it for business purposes, You have the right to request such categories of information sold or disclosed.
- **The right to opt out.** You have the right to direct businesses that sell or share Personal Data about You to third parties to stop such sales or sharing, known as the right to opt out. If You are a minor, this becomes

a right to opt in to the sale or sharing of data (exercised by the minor if You are between 13 and 16 years of age, or by the minor's parent or guardian if You are under 13 years old). Businesses must wait at least 12 months before asking You to opt back in.

- **The right to request deletion.** You also have the right to request deletion of Personal Data, but only where that information was collected from You. Like the right to erasure under the GDPR, this right is subject to exceptions. For instance, businesses need not delete Personal Data necessary for detecting security incidents, exercising free speech, protecting or defending against legal claims, or - in what is potentially a broad and likely contentious category - for internal uses reasonably aligned with Your expectations.
- **The right to limit use of Sensitive Personal Data.** You have the right to restrict a business' use of Sensitive Personal Data. For example, for the business to use Sensitive Personal Data as necessary to provide the goods or services requested, to certain business purposes, or other legally permitted purposes.
- **The right to equal services and prices.** Businesses must not discriminate against You by denying goods or services, charging a different price or rate for goods or services, providing a different level or quality of goods or services, or suggesting that they will do any of these things based upon Your exercise of any of Your legal rights relating to Your Personal Data. Put differently, You have a right to equal services and prices.
- **The right to appeal.** You have the right to appeal Our decision with regard to Your request to exercise any rights described herein.

If You would like to exercise any of Your rights under applicable law (including the right to appeal), please email [%_email_%].

Nevada Privacy

Your rights under privacy law in Nevada

Under this Privacy Policy, and by law if You are a resident of Nevada, You have the following rights:

We [%_do_or_do_not_%] sell Personal Data to third parties. Nonetheless, Nevada residents have a right to submit a request to opt-out of sale of Personal Data, referred to under privacy law in Nevada as "covered information." Upon receipt of a verified request, both as to the submission and the identity of You, we will ensure that no covered information, as defined under the privacy law in Nevada, is sold. We will further notify the customer within 60 days after receipt that the request has been processed. At this time, Nevada residents can only submit this request by contacting us via email at [%_email_%].

Website

We have no plans to serve ads, but if we ever do, You can opt out of receiving ads that are personalized as served by our Service Providers by following our instructions presented on the Service:

- From Our "Cookie Consent" notice banner

The opt out will place a cookie on Your computer that is unique to the browser You use to opt out. If You change browsers or delete the cookies saved by Your browser, You will need to opt out again.

Mobile Devices

Your mobile device may give You the ability to opt out of the use of information about the apps You use in order to serve You ads that are targeted to Your interests:

- "Opt out of Interest-Based Ads" or "Opt out of Ads Personalization" on Android devices
- "Limit Ad Tracking" on iOS devices

You can also stop the collection of location information from Your mobile device by changing the preferences on Your mobile device.

"Do Not Track" Policy as Required by California Online Privacy Protection Act (CalOPPA)

Our Service does not respond to Do Not Track signals.

However, some third party websites do keep track of Your browsing activities. If You are visiting such websites, You can set Your preferences in Your web browser to inform websites that You do not want to be tracked. You can enable or disable DNT by visiting the preferences or settings page of Your web browser.

Your California Privacy Rights (California's Shine the Light law)

Under California Civil Code Section 1798 (California's Shine the Light law), California residents with an established business relationship with Us can request information once a year about sharing their Personal Data with third parties for the third parties' direct marketing purposes.

If You'd like to request more information under the California Shine the Light law, and if You are a California resident, You can contact Us using the contact information provided below.

California Privacy Rights for Minor Users (California Business and Professions Code Section 22581)

California Business and Professions Code section 22581 allow California residents under the age of 18 who are registered users of online sites, services or applications to request and obtain removal of content or information they have publicly posted.

To request removal of such data, and if You are a California resident, You can contact Us using the contact information provided below, and include the email address associated with Your account.

Be aware that Your request does not guarantee complete or comprehensive removal of content or information posted online and that the law may not permit or require removal in certain circumstances.

Children's Online Privacy Protection Act of 1998 (COPPA)

When it comes to the collection of Personal Data from children under the age of 13 years old, the Children's Online Privacy Protection Act (COPPA) puts parents in control. The U.S. Federal Trade Commission (FTC), the United States' consumer protection agency, enforces the COPPA Rule, which specifies what operators of websites and online services must do to protect children's privacy and safety online.

[%_We do not specifically market to children under the age of 13 years old._%]

California Residents Under Age 16

The California Privacy Law introduces parental consent obligations consistent with COPPA (as described above) for children under the age of 13. For children between 13 and 16 years old, the California Privacy Law imposes a new obligation to obtain opt-in consent from the child. Under the California Privacy Law, California residents under age 16 must enable an opt-in process so that no Sale of the minor's Personal Data can occur without actively opting-in to the Sale.

[%_We do not sell personal information._%]

Links to Other Websites

Our Service may contain links to other websites that are not operated by Us. If You click on a third party link, You will be directed to that third party's site. We strongly advise You to review the Privacy Policy of every site You visit.

We have no control over and assume no responsibility for the content, privacy policies or practices of any third party sites or services.

Changes to Privacy Policy

In order to keep up with changing legislation and best practice, we may revise this Privacy Policy at any time without notice by posting a revised version on this website. So please check back periodically so that You are aware of any changes.

Contact us

If You have any questions about this Privacy Policy or relating to our use of Your information, please email us at [%_email_%].